Mary Lavin

THE IRISH WRITERS SERIES
James F. Carens, General Editor

TITLE	*AUTHOR*
EIMAR O'DUFFY	Robert Hogan
J. C. MANGAN	James Kilroy
J. M. SYNGE	Robin Skelton
PAUL VINCENT CARROLL	Paul A. Doyle
SEAN O'CASEY	Bernard Benstock
SEUMAS O'KELLY	George Brandon Saul
SHERIDAN LEFANU	Michael Begnal
SOMERVILLE AND ROSS	John Cronin
STANDISH O'GRADY	Phillip L. Marcus
SUSAN L. MITCHELL	Richard M. Kain
W. R. RODGERS	Darcy O'Brien
MERVYN WALL	Robert Hogan
LADY GREGORY	Hazard Adams
LIAM O'FLAHERTY	James O'Brien
MARIA EDGEWORTH	James Newcomer
SIR SAMUEL FERGUSON	Malcolm Brown
BRIAN FRIEL	D. E. S. Maxwell
PEADAR O'DONNELL	Grattan Freyer
DANIEL CORKERY	George Brandon Saul
BENEDICT KIELY	Daniel Casey
CHARLES ROBERT MATURIN	Robert E. Lougy
DOUGLAS HYDE	Gareth Dunleavy
EDNA O'BRIEN	Grace Eckley
FRANCIS STUART	J. H. Natterstad
JOHN BUTLER YEATS	Douglas N. Archibald
JOHN MONTAGUE	Frank L. Kersnowski
KATHARINE TYNAN	Marilyn Gaddis Rose

BRIAN MOORE	Jeanne Flood
PATRICK KAVANAGH	Darcy O'Brien
OLIVER ST. JOHN GOGARTY	J. B. Lyons
GEORGE FITZMAURICE	Arthur E. McGuinness
GEORGE RUSSELL (AE)	Richard M. Kain and
	James H. O'Brien
IRIS MURDOCH	Donna Gerstenberger
MARY LAVIN	Zack Bowen
FRANK O'CONNOR	James H. Matthews
ELIZABETH BOWEN	Edwin J. Kenney, Jr.
WILLIAM ALLINGHAM	Alan Warner
SEAMUS HEANEY	Robert Buttel
THOMAS DAVIS	Eileen Sullivan

MARY LAVIN

Zack Bowen

Lewisburg
BUCKNELL UNIVERSITY PRESS
London: ASSOCIATED UNIVERSITY PRESSES

© 1975 by Associated University Presses, Inc.

Associated University Presses, Inc.
Cranbury, New Jersey 08512

Associated University Presses
108 New Bond Street
London W1Y OQX, England

Library of Congress Cataloging in Publication Data

Bowen, Zack R
  Mary Lavin.

  (The Irish writers series)
  Bibliography: p.
  1. Lavin, Mary, 1912–
PR6023.A914Z68 1975   823'.9'12   73–126002
  ISBN 0–8387–7762–7
  ISBN 0–8387–7701–5 pbk.

Printed in the United States of America

Contents

Chronology   9

Acknowledgments   11

Introduction   15

I   17

II   23

III   43

IV   59

Bibliography   73

Chronology

1912   Born June 11 in Walpole, Massachusetts, the only child of Thomas and Nora Lavin.

1921   Nora and Mary return to Ireland and settle in Athenry.

1922   Thomas returns to Ireland, first joining Nora and Mary in Athenry. Later the family moves to Dublin where Mary attends the Loreto convent.

1926   Tom Lavin appointed Manager of Bective House.

1937   Mary's thesis on Jane Austen is accepted with honors at UCD after which she teaches French at Loreto convent.

1938   Mary Lavin visits the United States. First short story, "Miss Holland," published in *Dublin Magazine*.

1942   Mary Lavin marries William Walsh.
Publication of *Tales from Bective Bridge*.

1943   Mary Lavin is awarded the James Tait Black Memorial Prize.
Birth of daughter Valentine.

1944   Publication of *The Long Ago and Other Stories*.

1945   Publication of *The House in Clewe Street*.
Birth of daughter Elizabeth.

1946   Publication of *The Becker Wives and Other Stories.*
1947   Publication of *At Sallygap and Other Stories.*
1950   Publication of *Mary O'Grady.*
1951   Publication of *A Single Lady.*
1953   Birth of daughter Caroline.
1954   Death of William Walsh.
1956   Publication of *The Patriot Son and Other Stories.*
1957   Publication of *A Likely Story.*
1959   Publication of *Selected Stories.*
1959   First Guggenheim award.
1961   Publication of *The Great Wave and Other Stories.*
       Received the Katherine Mansfield Prize.
1960   Second Guggenheim award.
1964   Publication of *Stories of Mary Lavin.*
1967   Publication of *In the Middle of the Fields.*
1968   Received Honorary Doctor of Literature from UCD.
1969   Married Michael MacDonald Scott.
       Publication of *Happiness and Other Stories.*
1971   Publication of *Collected Stories.*
       Received the Ella Lynam Cabot award.
1972   Publication of *The Second Best Children in the World.*
1973   Publication of *A Memory and Other Stories.*

Acknowledgments

It is almost embarrassing to acknowledge my indebtedness to so many people for their substantial help in such a short critical introduction. However, the editorial and research contributions of Joseph Buttigieg, Barbara DiBernard and Marguerite Harkness were invaluable in the preparation of this essay, as were the careful readings of my colleagues, John Hagan and Sheldon Grebstein. Of course, the cooperation of Mary Lavin herself and Michael Scott made possible the biographical section and provided insights into the Lavin canon.

Mary Lavin

Introduction

This brief study is intended to provide what for most American readers will be an introduction to Mary Lavin and her works. Her stories have been accorded far less interest in the United States than they have in Ireland, and little critical material has appeared. In the only study of comparable length, an unpublished dissertation (University of Colorado, 1968), B. J. Roark discusses Lavin's thematic development. The present essay will include a biographical account, gleaned mostly from personal interviews with the author and her husband, an interpretation of her vision as reflected in her themes, and an analysis of her style, structure, and narrative perspective. I have chosen to conclude with a discussion of Lavin's two novels, not because they are her best works, but rather because they recapitulate most of the aspects of her themes and methods discussed earlier. The novels provide the opportunity for more detailed analysis, and the difference between the two novels indicates the range of Lavin's methods and themes.

Her early promise was recognized by Lord Dunsany in his introduction to *Tales from Bective Bridge*, in which he likens Lavin to the great Russian writers in her appreciation of people and her "astonishing insights." The quality and design of her writings have not substantially altered over the years. Her subjects have shifted slightly, with more widows in her stories now, but there are few other material changes in style or general content. Thus, early promise of greatness has given way to only partial fulfillment in Lavin's mature work. But the years and subsequent volumes have accumulated the substance from which a comprehensive perspective of the writer may now be formulated. Such is the intention of this essay.

I

Mary Lavin was born not in some quaint little Irish village, but in Walpole, Massachusetts, in 1912, to Thomas and Nora Lavin. Her father, originally from Roscommon, worked in Massachusetts for a wealthy American family. He met his future wife, Nora Mahon, as she was returning to Ireland from a visit to the United States. She was the daughter of a middle-class merchant in Athenry, but since there were twelve children in the family, money was not plentiful. Consequently, she was pleased to receive an invitation to visit her grand-uncle, the Reverend James Dermody, a parish priest in Waltham, Massachusetts. After she had been there for a time she found she disliked life in America. It was on the boat returning to Ireland that she met Tom Lavin, and three years later she went back to Boston to marry him. Thus, Nora was bound for years to live in the country she "loathed and detested." (All quotations in this chapter are from taped interviews of Mary Lavin, conducted by the author.) Even the birth of the Lavins' only child, Mary, and the distractions of raising an active little girl, could not allay Nora's desire to return home to Ireland and a life she under-stood.

Nora came from a lower middle-class family who regarded farmers and cattlemen of the sort with whom Tom Lavin made his living as somehow beneath them. In America she could not accustom herself to his way of life, and so she returned to Ireland with her daughter while Thomas remained as horse groom, chauffeur, and general caretaker of the Bird family property in Massachusetts. It was nearly a year before Tom Lavin also returned to Ireland.

Nora and her daughter went first to the home of Mary's grandparents in Athenry, where Mary, now nine, was sent to the local school. The eight months in Athenry left an indelible impression on Mary Lavin's work. She admits readily the influence the town had on her: "For years whenever I wrote a story, no matter what gave me the idea, I had to recast it in terms of the people of that town." Even experiences of her own became recast in her mind as the experiences of her aunts and uncles. Thus the town and family provided not only material for her fiction, but also a means of distancing her life from her work.

Nora and Mary left Athenry after Thomas succumbed to his wife's insistence that he send money for a house, and one was finally purchased in Dublin. No sooner were they in the house than Mr. Lavin decided he could no longer be away from his family or his new property. Accordingly, he joined them for a brief period before moving to Bective to assume management of a hunting estate Charles Bird had purchased there. Thomas Lavin seems to have had a strong influence on his daughter. He idolized her and lavished everything he could on his only child. And she responded with an obsessive devotion she seems to have carried through life. Her story "Tom" (*The New Yorker,* January 20, 1973) contains a revealing history of the relations of the Lavin family as well as portraits of her parents.

Once in Dublin, Mary was enrolled in the Loreto convent, where an older sister of one of the girls introduced her to *The Mill on the Floss*, and "that was the end of school stories." However, Tom Lavin often grew impatient with the pedantry of his daughter's education. On sunny days he would plague the sisters by insisting that she be brought from class so that they might take a walk together. Until much later the formal schooling of his daughter was never a matter of great importance to him. In spite of this disdain for education on the part of her father, Mary excelled both in studies and in extracurricular activities. She won the Bishop's Medal for Christian Doctrine, was captain of the debating team, and took at least one first place in English.

At University College, Dublin she was at first a timid student and not especially outstanding until the end of her college career. Then she won first honors in English and stayed on to write an M.A. thesis on Jane Austen which was also awarded first-class honors. Later, she abandoned a doctoral dissertation on Virginia Woolf in favor of her creative work.

After graduation, she returned for two years to the Loreto convent as a French teacher. During this period she married a former classmate, a Dublin lawyer named William Walsh, and when Thomas Lavin died they bought Mary's present home, The Abbey Farm, with the inheritance. The modern single-story house and adjoining service buildings of the farm lie along the Boyne. The home, never quite finished, is nevertheless comfortable and spacious, with a large picture window which overlooks the adjacent fields and the Abbey, one of the best-preserved historical sites in Ireland. The family's residence was divided between Bective and Dublin, where William's legal practice was conducted. Mary's limited time, occupied by their three children, Elizabeth, Valentine, and Caroline, and the farm, left her only a few odd moments for writing. As a result she found that the short story was the form most congenial to her and really the only one feasible in her circumstances. "With not much time to write, I had to write with great intensity, and the novel isn't an intense medium."

In 1953 William became seriously ill, and in the following year he died. After his death Mary was faced with difficult times and three children to raise. During that period she developed a terrible insecurity about money, a condition from which she has never been able to free herself. Because raising the children alone in reduced circumstances placed her writing time under even more stringent constraints, for five years her productivity was greatly impaired. Then she received Guggenheim awards in 1959–60 and in 1960–62. During the first award period, she packed up the children and went to Florence, where at first she was far worse off than at home. Three lively children on the loose in hotels and pensions made severe demands on their mother's time, and the family had little money. She received a renewal from the Guggenheim Foundation and decided to spend the next year at home, where the children could play in the fields and fiscal problems were not so pressing. In that year she wrote most of the stories in *The Great Wave* and *In the Middle of the Fields*.

The Guggenheim award provided the encouragement she needed to carry on, because after her husband died she had begun to doubt her ability to write. Now publication followed publication, and teaching offers came from colleges in the United States. Although she took the children to the continent every summer, she did not want to interrupt their schooling to take overseas jobs. However, she did accept invitations to read her works in the United States; and later, when the children were older, she served for several semesters as writer in residence at the University of Connecticut.

In 1969 Mary married her present husband, Michael Scott, a friend of many years, who left the Jesuit Order to marry her. She first met him the day she began as a student at University College. He was a first-year Jesuit student, and had arrived from Australia only the night before on the mail boat. They became very close, but agreed that his duty to the Order came first. When Scott was ordained he returned to Australia, and Mary fell in love with and married William Walsh. After Walsh died, and financial problems arose, Michael Scott was extremely concerned about Mary's well-being. They began to correspond regularly, and Father Scott applied for laicization. When it was granted six months later, they were married in a Jesuit chapel.

As Scott is now the Dean of the School of Irish Studies, the family divides its residence between their small Mews house in Dublin and Bective Abbey, where their cattle graze the Abbey's meadows.

The Abbey Farm, Mary's daughters, her widowhood and subsequent marriage, like many of her other personal experiences, come down to her readers transformed into fiction by her craft and imagination. Her stories are of people like herself and her neighbors, her settings local and realistic rather than remote and exotic. The vitality with which she has lived is reflected in her characters by an intensity which complements the beauty of their natural surroundings and sometimes contrasts with their restrictive society and the drabness of their personal lives.

II

Given Mary Lavin's lifelong concern with practicalities, money problems, responsibilities, and the effects of death, her vision of reality is harsh and closely circumscribed by an acute awareness of social class, and society's sanctions and rules. This is more than merely the theme of some of her stories; it is the donnée of her plots as well as the context of motive and constraint which condition the behavior of most of her characters. In the tightly controlled, sometimes fatalistic sphere in which her characters live, many of them succumb to a life of quiet frustration or desperation, while others try to escape, to rationalize, to hide, or to seek freedom through love, nature, insanity, or death.

Freedom, or the lack of it, then, is the all-pervasive theme of Lavin's work as her characters attempt to cope with their captivity. Other themes are merely incidental or contributory. For instance, "The Patriot Son," the only treatment of Irish nationalism in the Lavin canon, is really about matriarchy and personal liberation. Matty, a shopkeeper's son, has been admonished by his loyalist mother to do nothing that would seem treasonable to England. When his nation-

alist friend, Sean, is cornered in the shop by the authorities, Matty tries to throw the police off the scent by
donning Sean's coat and attempting to escape out the
back. The elation he feels when a sharp pain strikes
him and blood begins to flow is the elation of liberation
from the yoke of his mother's tyranny rather than
elation over the liberation of his country. The idea
that servitude, both domestic and national, seems
decreed by the fates becomes apparent when the mother
comes out in the backyard calling her son, who, far
from being shot, has only a gash from some rough
metal. Matty seems destined to the anonymity of
being a bystander in the nationalistic struggle and to
the ignominy of being a mama's boy in his shop. The
struggle for national independence, while providing
the exciting moments in the story, is little more than a
vehicle for the character analysis of a young man for
whom even death represents a welcome relief from the
dismal existence which has been his lot.

The personal afflictions which Lavin's characters
endure run the gamut from loneliness in "Miss Holland," "The Long Ago," "In the Middle of the Fields,"
"Heart of Gold," and many other stories, through the
tyrannies of older sisters or relatives in such stories as
"Frail Vessel," "The Little Prince," "The Will," and
"A Gentle Soul," to the unbearable conflicts of marriage in "At Sally Gap," "A Cup of Tea" and "The
Convert." Along with personal problems Lavin's characters often have to deal with poverty and, even more,
with an inflexible social order and caste system, so well
defined and predictable that Lavin can often treat a
town collectively as a character. It is of course possible
to do that in as closed a society as a village in central

Ireland, where many of Lavin's stories take place. "A Fable" is a prime example. Like Faulkner's "A Rose for Emily," the story develops the attitudes of the town toward a woman whom it despises for her beauty, venerates when the beauty becomes marred in an accident, and then regards ambivalently when the townsfolk think of her healing plastic surgery as temporary.

The rules are Victorian, mean, and all-pervasive. There is no mercy for those who violate them, attempt to evade them, or have pretensions above their station. Only rarely in Lavin's tales, as in the story "Posy," does the protagonist rise above his or her assigned station in life. Although Posy was a servant, her figure is nearly legendary in the mind of a shopkeeper who confesses his youthful romance with her to a young stranger. Since the young, well-dressed listener had asked originally for Posy's house, we early suspect, and later have our suspicions confirmed, that he is Posy's son. This situation provides dramatic irony for the older man's recounting how he and his sisters had regarded Posy as beneath them and how, since she had so obviously risen in the world, he had been the un-witting victim of his own middle-class snobbery.

More often the fate of those with social pretensions is ignominy and disgrace. The servants in "The Joy Ride," who take their master's horse and buggy when nobody is home, return to a house in ashes and certain punishment. Another servant, Magenta, in a story of the same name, assumes her mistress's airs along with the lady's illicitly borrowed clothes. The latter story is in many ways a social allegory, in which Magenta is befriended by two other domestics whose lack of spe-

cific supervision has also led them to adopt airs and
attitudes of owners rather than servants. Their attitudes are, however, staid, respectable, and except for
a little fling at getting their fortunes told, perfectly in
harmony with the social order. Magenta is, by contrast,
young, exuberant and wildly romantic. Like all young
romantics in Mary Lavin's books and stories, she will
suffer for her folly, as she proceeds to certain dismissal
for failing to return the clothes before discovery.

Still another story of servants overstepping their
prerogatives has exactly the same outcome. "The Small
Bequest" describes how two ladies, one a paid com-
panion-housekeeper to the other, are nearly inseparable
in life though the companion annoys her employer by
addressing her as "Aunt Adeline" when they are not,
in fact, related. The old lady gets her revenge by leaving the money to her companion, but designating the
younger woman her "niece," Emma, so that the companion can't touch it under the law.

Lavin employs even children to depict the social
class theme of the overly ambitious servant. "Scylla
and Charybdis" is a character study of a little steward's
daughter who seeks acceptance into the family of her
father's employers, two upper-class ladies. Pidgie's
big moment comes when she is asked to share some food
with one of the ladies, but then finds that she is expected to eat it in the servants' quarters. As she sticks her
tongue out at her benefactors, her state of rebellion may
very well reflect Lavin's own. Mary's father was a
steward, and her description of Pidgie sounds much like
what I imagine the writer to have been. It is safe to
surmise that much of Lavin's preoccupation with servants and social class strictures probably originated

in her mother's sense of Tom Lavin's lowered social status, despite the fact that he was later moderately successful as manager of the Bird estate.

Lavin's sense of social rigidity involves not only class distinctions, but, of course, the whole pattern of one's actions and life. The strictures put on Lavin's characters are harsh and the sanctions include even death. For example, "Sarah" is a tale of a temptress who scandalizes the community by seducing men and having illegitimate children. While the author does not condemn her libertine ways, Sarah does meet her end in a roadside ditch, after having been cast out of her brother's house. In Lavin's world vengeance is swift in overtaking those whose motive is passion rather than social dicta. In this story we are astonished at the sophistication of the betrayed wife who manages to control the situation and punish without doing anything that appears on the surface to be vindictive. Of course, she doesn't have to. She has the social order working for her, and all that is needed is just to create the bare suspicion of Sarah's guilt.

A frequent motif in stories such as "A Gentle Soul," "The Little Prince," "The Patriot Son" and "The Becker Wives" is the use of the social order by dominant relatives to impose a tyranny over another member of the family. However, in two of the most interesting variations on the motif the tyranny fails. "The Will" is a study of a youngest sister who has pursued her own way of life, marrying against her family's will and opening her house to boarders after her husband dies, again enraging the family by the public disgrace of her occupation as a landlady. When she comes home to her mother's funeral, to listen patiently to the ad-

monishments of her brothers and sisters and to learn
that her mother has willed her nothing, she submits
with quiet dignity to the insults. In leaving town she
only pauses at the priest's to spend her meager resources
for masses for her mother's soul, so frightened is she
of the mother's sinfulness in dying with such hatred
on her conscience. The act of worrying about her
mother, to the point of depriving herself and her now
fatherless family of food so as to offer masses for her
mother, strikingly demonstrates her conviction of the
rightness in what she has done; at the same time it
proves her love and charity for her carping, self-righ-
teous family.

The second story, "A Single Lady," takes up the
Electra theme of the girl who remained single to take
care of her father only to have him lavish his attention
on another woman in his dotage. Even more unseemly
are the social implications of her father's behavior with
the buxom lower-class servant. Capitalizing on the
disgust of the town when it is bruited about that a
marriage is imminent, the daughter tries to shock the
two by telling an allegorical story about lust in old age
and a servant's greed in accepting an old man's advances in order to inherit his money. She verbalizes
for the first time what they all have been thinking but
what to the daughter's surprise seems perfectly acceptable to the lovers. It is ironic that in the two best-written
stories involving the motif, dominance is not achieved
by relatives utilizing the sanctions of social propriety.
However, in the majority of Lavin's stories society *is*
the source of familial power, a condition much closer
to the norm if less interesting. The weight of this social
and religious order prompts moments of wild flight

and passionate rebellion in even the gentlest of characters. There is more Ethan Frome than Heathcliff in most of the seemingly tractable types who inhabit the writer's small Irish villages. In archetypal rites of passage, innocent youngsters like Mona in "Sunday Brings Sunday" are led to the full realization of the oppressions of social and religious maxims through their own violations of the order and the inevitable punishment, in Mona's case pregnancy. In this story Lavin renders the recognition in vibrant terms which communicate the hysteria of entrapment:

"Sunday Brings Sunday." Where was that voice? Was Mass over? Mona couldn't see well, but she could hear feet moving and she could hear the hag's voice shrilling in her ear. The feet were the feet of the year! The year was coming! The year was rushing up the rutty graveled yard. It was rushing in over the splintered wooden floor and grating on the flagstones where the dead priests of the parish were buried. It made a sound like the sound of a million feet, but it had only one blunt leg. She knew that. Ha! she knew that. She could see it even though she had her fists dug into her eyes. The year was a hobbled old hag! It was climbing over the pews. It was on top of her! It was skipping the Mondays and skipping the Thursdays and hopping from Sunday to Sunday. The Sundays were a lot of lice-eaten pews. It didn't take long to hop over them. . . .

The chapel was dark and getting darker and darker every minute. The darkness was like water and suddenly she was floating on it like the weeds that flowed on the ditches. But the ditches were cool and green, and she flowed in some dark water that was dirty and yellow and warm like hay. (*Collected Stories,* Boston, 1971)

Unlike James Joyce, Lavin does not normally portray religion or the Catholic Church *per se* as a trap. Rather it is the practical application of the religious institutions in the everyday domestic and social life of the characters that brings pain. For instance, the mixed marriages of the Lavin canon all seem to carry attendant trials. In "The Convert," the religious differences in a mixed marriage are so pervasive that they are largely unspoken by the characters who attribute to other causes their wretched life together.

Even the slings and arrows of a morally outraged village are to be preferred to the horror of a volitional mixed marriage. In "An Akoulina of the Irish Midlands," when a Protestant girl tells her Catholic suitor that she has gone to a priest in a nearby parish to receive religious instruction, he is outraged, preferring to take her off into the woods to "let things take their course," presumably toward a shotgun wedding:

" . . . you'd never know, they might be glad enough to have us getting married one of these days; they mightn't mind what sacrifices had to be made" (*The Patriot Son and Other Stories*, London, 1956).

Nor will a lifetime together substantially ease the pressures upon a couple where there is a difference in religion. In "The Lost Child," a woman decides to become a convert after years of marriage to a Catholic husband. When she has a miscarriage on the day of her public conversion, she inevitably links the two events with her sense of guilt about her dead child who is about to enter the limbo of Catholic doctrine as a punishment for her conversion.

Marriages in the Lavin vision are plagued by far

more than mere religious differences, however. Stories like "A Cup of Tea" depict hopeless marriages of un-relieved hostility. More often in her stories, the ennui of years of married life generates not only rancor and quiet desperation but also some search for escape. With the gentler characters of these stories, dramatic renunciations or sudden abandonments are not even considered alternatives. Rather, more socially ac-ceptable means of escape are sought—for example, in memory or sublimation. In the story "At Sallygap," as a case in point, the glories of natural surroundings in the open vistas of Sallygap contrast with the narrow confines of life in an apartment behind a Dublin shop. The trip to Sallygap recalls for the protagonist the promise of adventure in Paris, which he surrendered for a life of servitude to a barb-tongued, shrewish wife, while his dashed hopes floated under the Dunleary pier with the broken strings of his fiddle bow.

Throughout the Lavin canon nature worship is a frequent but seldom completely successful antidote for the frustrations of societal and psychological as well as domestic problems. In "Brother Boniface," the title character, well beyond eighty, has wanted only to worship nature and the God who has filled it with such wonder. From an early age, forced to struggle in his father's store, he turns to the monastery because he thinks he sees a monk there worshipping the stars and contemplating nature. It later appears the monk was only performing the Holy Office of the day. Ironically, Boniface becomes the busiest monk in the monastery, never stopping to do the things he came for, even in his old age when he must spend his time shooing the cat out of the flower bed. His life is spent in gentle, dumb—even unknowing—despair, his escape into nature only momentary and fleeting.

Even when Lavin's characters are given the opportunity to spend their lives close to the nature they adore, societal mores and concerns pervert and transform nature into an enemy rather than a sanctuary. In "The Haymaking," Fanny, a Dublin schoolteacher who has dreamed of a life in the country, wakes up after her honeymoon with her farmer-husband to find him changed into a kind of brute whose perversity is a hatred of the nature that sustains him. In her eyes, however, nature is glorious:

> Outside the early summer sun was already up over the rim of the sky, illuminating the countryside with the rich slanting rays that, like the evening rays, deepen the colour of the earth and enrich the glow of the grasses. In front of the house, but on the other side of the river, there was a field of meadow and upon the tops of the grasses the sun rays shone with a rich intensity, till the ryegrass and timothy and the top stalks of the tremble-grasses glowed like red copper. (*The Long Ago and Other Stories*, London, 1944)

She can feel this way because she is not yet really a farmer's wife. But nature merely threatens the farmer who can brook no rain as he harvests his crop of hay. Christopher, who was expected to marry a local farm girl with a properly realistic anti-nature attitude, repeats the refrain that his is not a proper farm wife. Later, when Fanny's sister comes to visit, the sister's love of nature begins to contrast with Fanny's newly learned pessimism about natural phenomena. As they travel toward the farm from the train station, Christopher takes all the credit for his bumper crop, and his wife— quite properly for a farm wife—begins what will become her lifelong litany against God and his weather: " 'It doesn't look too good this morning. The sky is so low you could reach it with a stick!' "

In other stories, however, such as "In the Middle of the Fields," nature, especially the fields of Meath, poses a counter motif to the adversities of societal, domestic and religious repression, engendering a sense of solitude and the joy of a life close to God.

The attempt of Lavin's characters to escape the oppressions that beset them takes many forms, extending even to madness. The story "The Becker Wives" is a study in schizophrenia about a wealthy merchant family whose money has purchased neither social distinction nor a sense of individuality. The youngest brother, Theobald, who sees his family as stolid, squat, unromantic, greedy, coarse, and unimaginative, tries to remedy the situation by bringing a glamorous, high-strung young woman into the family as his wife. Chief among Flora's gifts is her talent for mimicry, with which she brightens the lives of the Beckers.

The story treats the nature of reality and how the make-believe world of Flora Becker's impersonations captivates the rest of the family by making their lives seem different. Because one brother, Samuel, empathizes with Flora and she finds him more compatible than her own husband, her mimicry centers largely on Samuel's wife, Honoria. Just as the Beckers try to emulate Flora's fashionable eccentricities, her imitation of Honoria becomes obsessive. It is ironic that the seem-

ingly original character of Flora at the beginning is
at the end only a replica of the stolid but real character
of Honoria, who is anything but original and vital.

At the end, we learn of a history of mental illness in
Flora's family. Her schizophrenia really represents
for her an embrace of comfortable, sane, solid middle-
class values: pregnancy and propriety. In the last
paragraph, the reminders of her former glamour and
its relation to mundane existence are a recapitulation
of the theme of the inescapability of one's fundamental
life style.

> But when in exhaustion at last Flora rested against
> him, her weight was so light that he started; it was as if
> she had begun already to dissolve again into the wraithlike
> creature of light and air that had first flashed upon them
> in all its airy brilliance on the night of his own betrothal
> party, a spirit which they in their presumption had come
> so erroneously to regard as one of themselves; just one
> other of the Becker wives like Julia or Charlotte or the
> real Honoria. (*The Becker Wives and Other Stories*, Lon-
> don, 1946)

In Lavin's imagined but not-so-fictive world, the
ultimate escape from such oppressions as I have described is, of course, death, but since Lavin and most of
her characters are Irish Catholics, suicide seldom represents an attractive alternative. Nevertheless, Lavin
is preoccupied with death, and the effect of death upon
the living is perhaps the most frequent motif in her
writing. In one guise or another, death appears in
her stories as the inescapable absolute against which the
characters make their tentative decisions about the
conduct of their own lives. Following Lavin's own

widowhood, she wrote a number of stories with bereaved protagonists. Other stories compare attractions of living with those of dying, or consider the social aspects of death.

In earlier Lavin stories death seems preferable in many ways to the continuance of suffering in life. In "The Dead Soldier" a mother, grieving for her dead son, waits up at night for his ghost, and, when a neighbor comes to check the house, thinks that the ghost has indeed arrived. The final image of the story portrays not the grotesqueness of the dead son's ghost but rather the living appearance of the mother in whom youth and life are more horrible than death.

> The mask broke up at once, but when Solly went downstairs it formed again over the old face, stretching the skin until every wrinkle was flattened out, and giving the face a distorting appearance of youth, more terrifying than the face of death. (*Tales from Bective Bridge,* Boston, 1942)

In a comic variation on the death-over-life theme, "A Visit to a Cemetery" couples the appeal of death with the class-consciousness motif discussed earlier. The trip of the title suggests to two sisters the horrors of death. But their dread gives way to joyous anticipation as their thoughts of being buried with their as yet unnamed husbands leads to pleasant speculations of anticipated marriages and an afterlife in a more fashionable cemetery than the one in which their mother is interred. With light hearts, they proceed to the newer cemetery to discuss their futures.

Lavin usually uses the act of dying as a vehicle for

describing the process of living. If death is preferable
to life, it is because the constraints of life—domestic,
social and religious—no longer confine or inhibit,
so that in the presence of death we can often see how
life should have been lived. In "A Happy Death,"
perhaps the best of all the Lavin stories, this message
is clear to the reader, though not to the surviving part-
ner of a long and anguished marriage. Again death
is linked to the domestic and societal motifs. The story
is, as its title suggests, a tragi-comedy about the privacy of a couple whose love for each other has been
perverted by the wife's almost maniacal fixation on
appearances. She fills their house with lodgers to
provide new clothes for her husband so that she may
later adorn the front bench with his resplendent person.
When he is demoted to janitor in the library where he
works, they begin a war of nerves that goes on for years.
She wants to keep him home, huddled with their children in their damp, cold kitchen and slime-covered yard.
The husband is dying, presumably from tuberculosis,
and all he wants is some privacy with his wife, without
even his children, let alone the lodgers. He rails against
"Strangers! Strangers!" until he is finally taken to the
hospital to die. There a cataclysmic scene, Dostoyev-
skian in its intensity and strangeness, is played out as
an allegory of modes of approaching death. Another
man, an atheist and blasphemer, is dying in another
bed in the ward of this Roman Catholic hospital.
Shouting curses, he finally is converted by means of
visions of hell and fear of eternal punishment. His
last moments are of unspeakable terror and torment
for his soul. Meanwhile, the wife's preoccupation with
appearances and her love for her husband take the

form of buying decorative fruit and sweets to display on his night table, so that he'll have more than the other patients. When a nun tries to dissuade her from spending her money on such trash, by reminding her that she ought to be concentrating on her husband's soul, she arranges to have an inordinate number of masses and special intentions said for him so that he might recover consciousness and have final repentance and absolution before he dies. When the man in the other bed dies screaming with just those benefits, she becomes frenzied trying to get her husband, when he does finally regain consciousness for the last time, to recite acts of contrition. But all he can do is tell her how much he has always loved her, and how all he ever wanted was just to be alone with her. Thinking that he has gained this privacy at last, he dies with great peace and tranquillity, in contrast to his wife's hysteria:

> And as she was led out of the ward a few minutes later, she was still screaming and sobbing, and it was utterly incomprehensible to her that God had not heard her prayers, and had not vouchsafed to her husband the grace of a happy death. (*The Becker Wives*)

The couple spend their lives together, failing to understand each other, and ultimately destroying one another with perverted love. The happiness of the death is not only in the husband's emancipation from the social and religious tyrannies imposed by his wife, but also in his ultimate freedom from ever having to understand her. She, on the other hand, remains alive, caught in the grips of her own self-imposed torments.

Freedom from the constraints of accommodation to

domestic and social situations, then, confers upon the
process of dying an honesty which few of Lavin's
characters can maintain in their everyday lives. Death
has its advantages both in the afterlife of reconciliation
with loved ones and in leaving behind the falsities of
this world. "One Summer" treats the truth in dying
and the futility of life based on false values. The story,
reminiscent of Joyce's "Eveline," is about a dominant
father for whom his daughter sacrifices her potential
marriage and a trip to Australia with her suitor. Although she gives up her youth, joy, and even her sense
of humor for her father, his last exclamation in the
story is not about his daughter, but his wife, whom he
has hardly mentioned during his life with his daughter:

> "Just to see her! Just to see her!"
>   Vera's own eyes widened. "Who are you talking about?"
>   "Your mother," he said, and he looked surprised.
> "Who else?" (*In the Middle of the Fields*, London, 1967)

The story bears echoes of Michael Scott's sailing off to
Australia as well as Tom Lavin's deep effect upon his
daughter, as the various aspects of the author's own
life are transmogrified from the "foul rag-and-bone
shop" of her heart.

What emerges is a kind of allegory of loneliness
and human separation. Each person lives in his own
private world, interacting with and even loving others,
but at the same time entirely separate and removed
from them. Thus the father had loved only his wife all
along, without his daughter's knowledge. He had
retained all those years a secret memory unknown to
all around him, even his own daughter. Only death

with its attendant hope for a brighter second life reveals the bleakness of this one.

In only one story, however, is the question of whether it is better to be living or dead discussed directly, and the decision, grim as the alternatives are, is on the side of life. "A Tragedy" is set against the familiar motif of domestic discord and the unpleasantness among a married couple and the sister of the wife, who are forced to live together in an attitude of recrimination and hostility. The sister's homecoming occurs against thè background of an air crash, the details of which are on everyone's lips at the time. The fate of the dead is envied by one sister and, as the other sister speculates on the first's death wish, life, with all its tribulations, seems preferable:

> Not one of them—those undiscovered dead in their far-flung graves, not one of them, she knew, but would fling back, if he could, his mantle of snow and come back to it all: the misunderstandings, the worry, the tension and cross-purposes. (*The Patriot Son*)

So, life goes on and the sorrows of death provide a lens by which the living can discern truth and continue to exist. The story in which this is most succinctly demonstrated is "Grief," an allegory of sorrow from two different perspectives, that of a middle-aged man who has just lost his mother, and that of an old woman whose husband lies mortally ill in the hospital. The ways in which their grief operates demonstrate the contrast in their character. She is an extroverted, cliché-spouting individual and he an introspective, reticent man whose mother has shaped his ideas on

life with her homilies. While the old woman rants he
recalls his mother's exclamation, "Isn't life extra-
ordinary!" indicating her belief that life contains its
own intrinsic interest and value, resistant to tragedy
and suffering.

Much of Lavin's mature work is dedicated to this
principle. Her widows and widowers, like herself,
have to pick up the pieces of their lives and survive
somehow. That the experience with death has made
them at once vulnerable but stronger becomes apparent
in the fact that they nearly always emerge victorious
over the forces and obstacles in their paths. Nearly
the whole of an entire later volume, *In the Middle of
the Fields*, explores the strengths and weaknesses
resulting from confrontations with death. Published
together nearly thirteen years after the death of Mary
Lavin's first husband, the stories form a cohesive
collection of variations on the theme of the dead spouse.
Only two stories, "The Lucky Pair" and "The Mock
Auction," do not deal with dead mates. But the latter,
the last story in the collection, concerns a housekeeper's
attempt to run a farm after the death of the two principal owners. In sum, these stories deal with all aspects
of survival and the possible alternatives posed by the
death of someone close. The stories are really an allegory of perseverance, of despair giving way to hope.
It is as if Lavin herself had considered all the facets
of death, struggled with the possibilities of her own
future and that of her family, and was announcing a
triumph over her own problems.

The title story has as its protagonist an unnamed
woman whose helplessness and fear of being alone
with her children after dark provide an initial impression

of her inability to cope with the world. However, the reader soon realizes that she is a resourceful person who will no more be taken in by neighborhood hired hands than she will let herself be used amorously or become the victim of scandal or abuse. When the local man tries to delay cutting her field as he had promised, she keeps him to his word. When he tries to take advantage of the widow, and is shamed out of his lust and out the door, we realize that her defenses are more than adequate to meet any challenges to her survival.

Death, then, with its accompanying sorrow, truth, hardship, and ultimate strength, provides at least some of the answers to the dilemma of life in the tragic thematic vision of Mary Lavin. The constraints of social, domestic and individual circumstances create the plights of her characters, whose alternatives are either escape or perseverance. Of these two courses clearly the second is the bitter-sweet choice of the author. "Happiness," the title story of the most recent collection considered in this study (*A Memory and Other Stories* was not yet published at the time this essay was written), is one of the most nearly autobiographical of Lavin's stories. The protagonist is a widow with daughters and an admirer who is a priest. It is tempting to surmise that since the details are so close to her own life, the philosophy of happiness espoused by the widow is also Lavin's philosophy. First we learn what the idea does *not* embody:

> Her theme was happiness: what it was, what it was not; where we might find it, where not; and how, if found, it must be guarded. Never must we confound it with pleasure. Nor think sorrow its exact opposite. . . . "I've known

people to make sorrow a *substitute* for happiness. . . ."
(*Happiness and Other Stories*, London, 1969)

If the rest of this story is an anatomy of happiness, then I suppose happiness must be the widow's life itself, in which there is much sorrow and pain, much responsibility, and much to occupy every minute of her day. Her dying is an appreciation of all that made life worth living, and her last worries are that her flowers will be abused by the hospital nun and placed in an unnatural setting. The definition of happiness that seems to emerge from this story and Mary Lavin's own history and personality is an embrace of the joys and pains of life and an appreciation of their unique and memorable characteristics.

III

Although Mary Lavin has written two novels, her normative medium is the short story, in part, as she claims, because the time spans during which she writes are so limited, but in greater measure because her interest in character portraits and the limited actions which delineate them are more properly circumscribed within the confines of the short story. Lavin explains her own situation accurately in her introduction to *Selected Stories* (New York, 1959):

They imposed a selectivity that I might not otherwise have been strong enough to impose upon my often feverish, overfertile imagination. So if my life has set limits to my writing I am glad of it. I do not get a chance to write more stories than I ought; or put more into them than ought to be there.

But how much is that? I think I begin to know. I even wish that I could break up the two long novels I have published into the few short stories they ought to have been in the first place. For in spite of these two novels, and in spite of the fact that I may write other novels, I feel that it is in the short story that a writer distills the essence of his thought. I believe this because the short story, shape as well as matter, is determined by the writer's

own character. Both are one. Short-story writing—for
me—is only looking closer than normal into the human
heart. The vagaries and contrarieties there to be found
have their own integral design.

In her statement, Mary Lavin alludes to one of the
most striking characteristics of her work: her intensely
personal, autobiographical approach to her stories.
As I have already suggested, there can be little doubt
that most of the experiences of her characters are drawn
from the experiences of the author and her relatives,
friends and acquaintances. Most of the facets of her
life—her upbringing, her devotion to her father, her
mother's early fascination with a Protestant suitor,
her matriarchal approach to life, her Roman Catholi-
cism, her family of shopkeepers, her middle-class background, her life in Dublin, Meath and particularly
Trim and Athenry, and the hardships of her widowhood—comprise the materials she shapes into her
fictional picture of life.

That this picture has such verisimilitude is partially
due to her style, which is normally purely functional
and rarely calls attention to itself. Her writing is perfectly clear and lucid, undistinguished by eccentricities
and seldom characterized either by excesses or by
habitual patterns of words or phrases. The advantages
and disadvantages of this become immediately clear.
Like the organic style of realism, Lavin's prose affords
an attitude of scientific impartiality, enhances the verisimilitude of the situation described and distances the
author from the content, while at the same time the
absence of idiosyncrasies makes the stamp of her own
genius more difficult to ascertain and describe.

There are a few exceptions, however. Occasionally the directness of the prose is played off against the vagaries of dialect to produce desired effects. For instance, "The Green Grave and the Black Grave" contains an unearthly islands' dialect which lends supernatural or legendary overtones to the love story. The dialogue contains repetitive refrain lines which suggest an analogy between the action and a ballad.

> "This is a man that will be missed mightily," said Tadg Beag.
> "He is a man that will be mightily bemoaned," said Tadg Mor.
> "He is a man that will never be replaced."
> "He is a man that will be prayed for bitterly and mightily." (*Tales from Bective Bridge*)

The language reenforces the tone of romantic desperation which pervades the story when the fishermen who discover Eamon Og Murnan's body later discover that his wife has gone out to share his fate with him, rather than, like the more staid island women, merely sitting ashore and bemoaning her loss. The unearthly dialogue, in a sense like that of *Riders to the Sea*, moves the story with a cadence which contrasts startlingly with the flat clarity of the narration to give the essentially domestic tragedy romantic and even Gothic proportions.

A second major departure from Lavin's stylistic norm occurs in her children's stories in which the style is adapted to the readers' age level. Her first story written for children, *A Likely Story*, differs stylistically from Lavin's usual straightforward prose by its eloquence of diction and metaphor:

Do you know Bective? Like a bird in a nest, it presses close to the soft green mound of the river bank, its handful of houses no more significant by day than the sheep that dot the far fields. But at night, when all its little lamps are lit, house by house, it is marked out on the hillside as clearly as the Great Bear is marked out in the sky. And on a still night it throws its shape in glitter on the water. (*A Likely Story*, New York, 1957)

Though the story begins, "Once upon a time . . . ," its tone is never really condescending nor is it patronizing in its moral attitudes. While the same freedom from the moral bludgeon is mercifully missing from Lavin's other children's story, *The Second Best Children in the World*, its style is intended for very young children and stresses rhymes and some words printed in inexplicably large type. These featured utterances seem much easier than others which do not appear in such large print. Obviously the book has some educational theory behind it, but the nature of the theory escapes me.

Other lapses from Lavin's customarily unobtrusive style are few. Where such deviations do occur they support a special effect, usually a comic effect. Occasional forays into bombast or effusiveness generally signal a light, humorous tone to the story. An example of this is "The Bunch of Grape" in which two little girls are sent to the store to buy grapes for an afternoon social. The voluptuous quality of the prose underlines the magnitude of the trial the little girls undergo when they attempt to bring the grapes home uneaten. The sensuous description of the delectability of the grapes recalls the temptation of Adam:

Blue Dress opened the bag again and drew out the beautiful grape. With them arose the wavering ribbons of vinous odour. She held them high over her head. They shone. They swelled. They pulsed with light. They revealed to her, and the covetous sun, their veined but bloodless flesh. (*The Long Ago*)

The uninhibited way in which the girls embrace sin once the dam of righteousness has broken seems humorously justified by the magnitude of the temptation, the proportions of which could only be communicated by the extravagance of the prose.

Indeed, despite the emphasis I have given to tragic themes, Mary Lavin's work is often very funny. It is not unusual to find a writer with so serious a vision as hers able to accommodate a grim outlook in black humor. Much of Lavin's humor is of the gallows variety; however, there is also much which is genuinely exuberant. Lavin's humor runs the gamut from robust ribaldry, through more subtle situations and black humor, to the light humor of her stories for and about children. A few examples are enough to indicate the varieties. "Lilacs," for instance, opens with a long comical dissertation on dung heaps. The dependence of Molloy on dung collecting for a living typifies Lavin's robust humor, as well as the conflict which underlies much of her work, that is, between the ideal, represented by the lilacs of the title, and the realities of the world, exemplified by the dung to which one after another of the family turns for a living. Stacey, the most ardent advocate of removing the smelly substance and planting lilacs instead, is left in the last line of the story with the same problem the former heads of the Molloy household faced: "But what will you live on, Miss Stacey?"

An example of Lavin's slapstick humor again embodies a dialectal departure from her usual straightforward prose, this time to reenforce the comic aspects of her story. "My Vocation" is a first-person narrative by a lower-class Dublin girl, about her brush with the convent. With an unmistakable ring of authenticity in both dialect and manner, this sensual girl relates with comic solemnity her tale of how nuns from the foreign missions come to her house to recruit her. When the nuns' carriage breaks down and their feet dangle through the floor of the runaway vehicle, they hear only screams of derisive laughter from their prospective novice. The result is that the girl escapes a life of religious devotion in the slapstick scene which climaxes the anecdote.

Appropriately, most of Lavin's black humor deals with death and interment. We have already discussed "A Visit to the Cemetery" with its comic mood of anticipation. The comic aspects of incarceration climax another blackly humorous story involving the social mores of a town which has its sensibilities offended by the sensual behavior of two of its citizens. "Loving Memory" is a funny, risqué story of a husband and wife who are always upstairs together, neglecting everything else but each other. The straight-laced husband, who has never flirted like his sisters' beaux, goes at married life with a vengeance:

> "And to think," cried Ellen, "that when he was a young fellow, no one thought he'd ever marry, much less take

to it like another man would take to drink." (*The Great Wave and Other Stories*, London, 1961)

Alicia, the young bride, behaves scandalously despite the speculation of the village that she would be both old and dull. The couple flouts convention and shocks the town by taking their honeymoon at home, and for years rarely leave their room, despite the children and the miscarriages that result. The only time they do leave is at night for walks, when Alicia carries a vaginal-symbol muff that links both their hands together. When she dies, Mathias, her husband, is almost grotesquely concerned that she receive a proper monument of just the right material and size so that it will be unique and she will be remembered by all. He goes to the cemetery night after night to measure the light and shadows that a tombstone would cast on her grave in the moonlight. This morbid fascination leads the townspeople to threaten their tardy children with the admonition, "Alicia Grimes will get you!" This story of love and memory, caricatured by the townsfolk into something sinister, is a masterful, perfect blend of ludicrous, realistic, and ironical elements.

Lavin's stories for and about children inevitably elicit the author's lighter side. The comedy in Lavin's stories written for children lies not so much in the situations as in the style. Stories involving children, however, such as "The Bunch of Grape," exploit thematically both the foibles of children and the adults around them. "A Glimpse of Katey," for instance, relates a little girl's fears of the dark, her attraction to the gay time her mother and sisters are having singing downstairs after she and her father have gone to bed,

and her precocious repetition of her father's grousing
about all the noise: "Disgraceful! Disgraceful!" (*The
Patriot Son*). In another story involving children,
"The Long Holidays," the brunt of the humor is
borne not by a child but by a woman who marries a
widower and labors to prepare the house for her stepson's holidays, only to find her floors scratched by
his hobnailed boots, her meals spoiled by his wart-
covered hands, and her sensibilities assailed by his
story of a classmate who removes the blemishes by
biting them off. As the stepson's outrages mount in
intensity to his climactic anecdote about his talented
classmate, the enormity of his offense to her delicate
sense of decorum increases, and with it the mirth of
the narrative.

Lavin's humor, in keeping with her characteristic
stylistic method, is generally unambiguous and straightforward. It is not surprising, therefore, that her use of
images follows the same unobtrusive pattern, with
heavy reliance upon dramatic metaphor, in which
specific images are important because they have meaning to the characters themselves. In contrast to D. H.
Lawrence's characters, who are often given to lengthy
discursive statements about the meaning of objects
and events, Lavin's characters are more engrossed in
the process of living than in discussing that process.
If they do stop to think about the significance of events
in their lives, however, the things they single out tend
to become the central metaphors of their respective
histories. A good example of this occurs in "At Sallygap," already discussed briefly in terms of the escape
motif. Manny Ryan's decision to pass up a glamorous
life as a Paris musician for the certainties of domesticity

in Ireland becomes crystallized in the metaphor of his broken fiddle dropped into the water when it was thrown to the recalcitrant Manny by a departing musician:

> "Whenever I see that little boat," he said, "I get to thinking of the sea and the way it was that day, with all the dirt lapping up and down on it and the bits of the fiddle looking like bits of an old box. Walking back to the train, we could see the bits of it floating along on the water under us, through the big cracks in the boards. . . . And just as we were going out the gate to the platform, what did I see, down through the splits, but a bit of the bow. And here's a curious thing for you! You could tell what it was the minute you looked at it, broken and all as it was. 'Oh, look!' you'd say if you happened to be passing along the pier, going for a walk and not knowing anything about me or the boys. 'Look!' you'd say to whoever was with you. 'Isn't that the bow of a fiddle?'" (*Collected Stories*)

Such metaphorical associations once perceived by the character often transcend the significance of the action in progress. Occasionally the realization of the metaphor by a character shapes the course of future events in a story. "The Cuckoo Spit" is a prime example. In it a widow, seeking to recover from the loss of her husband, enters into a romance with another man. As the affair becomes more serious, the man must go to Dublin for a set of examination papers he is to grade, and he temporarily suspends the romance for the papers. When they rendezvous in Dublin and are about to return to the country together to spend the night, again the examination papers intervene. He asks that they stop by his apartment to pick them up and she, thinking better of their recklessness, drives away. Finally, when she really needs him to accompany her to the cemetery to care for her husband's tombstone, the examination papers intervene once again. This time the excuse seems even more ludicrous—he must give driving lessons to the Department of Education official who supplies him with the test papers. The recurrent, anti-romantic exam paper motif epitomizes the mundane reality the lovers face and undercuts the sentimentality which could easily develop from such a theme. Moreover, the story juxtaposes the image of the exam papers against that of the tombstone. The monument symbolizes the widow's loss and her need for the love and assistance she once received from her husband and which she is not likely to get from the would-be lover, whose ardor is tempered by the pragmatic priorities of his own life.

In other stories metaphoric motifs act more subtly upon the characters, sometimes subliminally. "Love Is for Lovers" is about a bachelor who is attracted and repelled by the warm sensuality of a shapely widow. When her advances to him indicate that some sort of marital commitment is necessary, he retreats to his damp, white bachelor bedroom. The story is informed by a color metaphor which contrasts the Widow Colligan's warmth and sensuality, represented by her affinity for the color orange, and the sterile coolness of white in which the bachelor takes refuge.

Where the central image is not directly a factor in crucial decisions by the characters, it often symbolizes or heralds those decisions. For instance, in the story "A Cup of Tea" a familiar Lavin theme, the souring over the years of a marital relationship, is embodied in the central metaphor of souring milk which the mother tries to salvage by boiling, just as she tries to remedy and palliate the souring of her marriage. The daughter, in refusing to drink the milk she knows has gone bad, foreshadows her ultimate judgment about the relationship between her mother and father.

Finally, Lavin uses incongruous images and metaphors to enhance comic or hyperbolic descriptions of characters and events. One memorable example of this is her metaphoric depiction, in "The Becker Wives," of the Becker family's diet.

> The fish however had gone the way of the soup and still there was no sign of Theobald, and soon the dinner was mid-way through its courses, or at least mid-way through its courses with regard to the number of dishes that had been consumed, although considering the nature of the courses, it might perhaps be said that the dinner was near its end, or rather that having successfully crossed the biggest of the fences, the guests were coming into the straight, and would gather speed now for the gallop home. In other words, having consumed the turtle soup, the curled whiting, the crown roast of young beef, accompanied by mounds of mashed potatoes, and little heaps of brussels sprouts, they might be expected to make quicker progress through the following and lighter dishes, the green salad and the peach melba, the sliver of anchovy on toast, the cheese crackers, the coffee and the *crème de menthe.*

The symbols in Lavin's stories are comparatively rare. Where they do operate they are functional, objective epitomes of the situations in which the characters find themselves. Accordingly, the metaphors often have significance both in and outside the story, to the characters as well as the readers. In the above excerpt from "The Becker Wives," the narrative point of view, though third-person omniscient, is largely that of Theobald, the dissident son whose original view of the family is one of embarrassed disgust.

The story embraces the normal narrative point of view for Lavin, selective omniscience. This narrative pattern is most obvious in Lavin's character vignettes. Many of her stories seek solely to present a character trait or portrait through an action which will enhance its development. In doing so Lavin has created a remarkable catalogue of characters such as Miss Holland, the Inspector's Wife, the Nun's Mother, the butlers of "A Joy Ride," the young nun of "Chamois Gloves," Pidgie, and the widow of "In a Cafe." In all of these cases the narrative point of view reflects the mind of the protagonist and in several stories approaches stream of consciousness.

Deviations from a third-person narrative pattern are comparatively few, and often these are stories which are so obviously autobiographical that Lavin drops the third person distancing for a more natural first-person narrative. "Tom," a story which recounts a little girl's relations to her parents, particularly her father, is a prime example. There is still the element of fiction even in those stories which seem purely autobiographical, but the emotions, if not the facts, have their counterpart in the author's life. "Story with a Pattern," to be discussed later, and "Say Could That Lad Be I?" are further examples of Lavin's involvement in her own stories: first, because they concern the nature of her art; and second, because the narrative point of view differs so remarkably from her normal perspective. The latter, "Say Could That Lad Be I?" is a first-person narration by the author remembering the voice of her father, who in turn recollects his boyish adventures with his dog. There is about the story the amorality of elders' tales of youthful derring-do, not the kind that Lavin herself would normally write. It is a father's story, and, as such, presumably holds a place in the author's heart sufficient to publish it along with her own more sophisticated fiction.

The author's involvement is thus natural to a first-person point of view. Where the involvement interferes with the impartiality of the third-person narration, it becomes a defect, however. Early in the author's career, there was an unfortunate tendency to violate the narrative perspective by pontificating or commenting upon the action. Happily, this has diminished over the years, but it was especially vexatious in "The Widow's Son" and "The Sand Castle." I will discuss the former presently, but the latter story contains several instances of sermonizing, one in particular where the violation of the detached narration is so blatant that it requires mention:

> When the artist first begins to shape his creation he is filled with a pride in himself and cannot bear to think that any hand but his could shape the perfection of the dream behind his brain, but as the dream emerges into a tangible form his selfish pride in his own power fades before a pure, unselfish pride in the thing he has created. Then he is willing and anxious to accept help from others, and is even ready, if necessary, to make the tragic ab-

negation of abandoning his task to other hands if those hands seem better fitted than his own to consummate the task. (*At Sallygap and Other Stories*, Boston, 1947)

This is, of course, the exception to normally even and consistent third-person narration.

There are few experiments in structure in the Lavin canon. Many of her stories are character vignettes in which the action is a mere vehicle for character revelation. Others, in which plot plays a more paramount role, often begin in *medias res*, with the ultimate details of the action informing the meaning of the characters who participate as well as the plot itself. An example of this is one of the most popular of Lavin's stories, "The Great Wave." The exciting details of the tragedy appear in a flashback in the mind of a bishop revisiting the island on which he and another youngster were the only survivors of the great wave. The story carries with it, because of this distancing of time, the attitude that the disaster may have been the work of divine providence. The realistic details of the frame and the disclosure of the identity of the bishop at the end lend both a sense of reality and a perspective of distance at the same time, putting the disaster in an historical context but preserving its immediacy.

In her one noteworthy departure from her own structural norms, "The Widow's Son," Lavin experiments with two equally plausible endings, one in which the son is killed and one in which he is not. Both are equally moving, though the second seems more traditionally tragic because the widow herself brings about the calamity by driving her son off with a public upbraiding for his running over a hen in the road rather than taking a tumble off his bicycle as he did in the first version. The widow's speech is prompted by her sensitivity to what her neighbors might think rather than the dictates of her heart, and this leads to ultimate misfortune. However, even this pathetic story of a victim of a deterministic social situation hardly requires the author's sermonizing at the end:

> Perhaps all our actions have this double quality about them; this possibility of alternative, and that it is only by careful watching, and absolute sincerity, that we follow the path that is destined for us, and, no matter how tragic that may be, it is better than the tragedy we bring upon ourselves. (*A Single Lady and Other Stories,* London, 1951)

Thus the author's justification for her experimental departure from the standard structure is the piece of didacticism so relentlessly expounded at the end. If there is a reason for plot, then let it be an instructive one!

Indeed, Lavin is exceptionally sensitive to the charge that her stories lack satisfactory resolutions. This was revealed in private conversation with her and more importantly in "A Story with a Pattern," cited by Augustine Martin ("A Skeleton Key to the Stories of Mary Lavin," *Studies* [Winter 1963]) as being "the closest the author ever gets to an artistic manifesto." The author, speaking in her own voice, tells how she is confronted at a party by a man who claims she has no plot in her stories.

> "And the endings," he said. "Your endings are very bad. They're not endings at all. Your stories just break off in the middle! Why is that, might I ask?" I'm afraid

that I smiled superciliously. "Life itself has very little plot," I said. "Life itself has a habit of breaking off in the middle." (*A Single Lady*)

He proceeds to tell her a story "with a plot" about a clubfooted man who precipitates his wife's death by accusing her of carrying another man's child. When she and her child both die, the stillborn infant has clubfeet. Without denying the obvious merits of the story, the narrator admits that it won't change her writing habits:

> "Because I won't always be able to find stories like this to tell. This was only one incident. Life in general isn't rounded off like that at the edges; cut into neat shapes. Life is chaotic; its events are unrelated."

Thus we have the Lavin defense: that her stories are slices of life and as a realistic writer she cannot re-manufacture life, which does not fall into neat little complete sequences. This defense has long been invoked by realistic writers. If it squared with the actual practice in all of Lavin's stories it would be perfectly adequate. However, it does not resolve the question of what happens to her stories-with-morals, or explain her editorializing.

IV

I have chosen to conclude this brief study with an analysis of Lavin's two novels because they embody most of the themes and stylistic and structural characteristics discussed previously. The failures of *Mary O'Grady* and the successes of *The House in Clewe Street* depend largely on the different ways in which the themes of a social code of behavior and social class system, with their concomitant mores and adversities, are dealt with by the characters in each novel. That Gabriel Galloway comes to an understanding of their meaning is a result of his struggle with and questioning of the code, leading to a balanced structure and acceptable resolution for the Clewe Street novel. On the other hand, Mary O'Grady's unquestioning acquiescence results not in any dramatic recognitions but rather in nearly unmitigated suffering so acute that the novel degenerates into near maudlin sentimentality of style as well as of theme. Mary's ultimate escape into the Elysian fields is both unsatisfying and unrealistic, while Gabriel's distress results in a realistic reappraisal of the world in which he lives and of his place in it.

Mary O'Grady is about a strong wife and mother

whose near faultlessness and acquiescence in the prevailing order at the beginning, middle and end of this long book leave her little essential to learn about herself, and nothing except fate to blame for her suffering and the evils that befall her and her family. The novel is a family epic, as we follow Mary through the birth of five children, the death of her husband and two of her daughters, the madness of her eldest son, the voluntary exile to Africa of her youngest son, and the shaky marriage of her surviving daughter. The book begins in Mary's youth, with the sacrifice of her cherished ancestral home in Tullamore for a cramped Dublin row house, and proceeds through an orgy of self-sacrifice culminating only when, still pining to see her beloved Tullamore, she unobtrusively expires. Her poverty, her pride, and her seemingly unerring sense of what is right save neither herself nor her children from a variety of domestic calamities.

She embraces completely and without question the dictates of the social and religious order which shapes her existence. For instance, when her oldest son Patrick returns from America penniless and driven mad by his misfortunes and is committed to an institution, she fears only for her younger son Larry's future, which will now be jeopardized because of the social stigma of his brother's instability. For a while she refuses to let Patrick be committed for the care he needs, because of its social stigma, and when Patrick is cured years later she is relieved to hear that he'll never be released, even though he is declared sane by the doctor. She is reconciled, doesn't want the responsibility, and doesn't want people to defame him. This healthy man is to be kept behind the walls of the asylum for the rest of his life; yet Mary doesn't seem to regret it. The moral question never becomes a conscious issue for her. The social order is not to be questioned. We see this obedience manifested in all Mary's judgments as well as in those of the offspring she has trained. Patrick must go to America as a second-class passenger rather than work his way across or travel steerage. Larry must have a new black suit for the seminary, Rosie a new dress, etc. When Larry later is expelled from the seminary just before ordination and is not sure what his course will be, he decides to become a missionary in Africa because he knows that will please his mother and avoid the public stigma of being "a spoiled priest." Finally, the only indication of Mary's impending death, aside from a pain in her shoulder, is her inability as her age advances to keep up appearances in the house, something that would never had happened if she were physically able to prevent it.

There are few lapses in the predominantly omniscient narrator style of *Mary O'Grady*. Rarely does Lavin violate the narrative perspective to address the audience directly as she does so often in *The House in Clewe Street*. Only once, when Larry comes home from the seminary, does the narrative change complexion to include a brace of biblical quotations and a spate of rhetoric about divine pupose. Perhaps it merely seems as if Mary O'Grady is near sainthood, because the selectively omniscient narrative focus remains on her. Her apparent gift of clairvoyance may be largely of her own making. For instance, when her children are young, she is obsessed by fear of their falling. When the two oldest girls finally do die in an air crash, her seemingly unsubstantiated earlier fears are vindicated.

Her reluctance to let Patrick, her oldest, go to America seems to be no more than the idle concern of an overly protective mother, but his return justifies her apprehensions. Her fears for Larry's chances of ordination prove entirely correct; and her admonishments to her daughter Rosie about Rosie's prospective husband are also borne out by the couple's unhappy marriage.

Finally, in the end, the weakest section of the novel, the narrative nearly grinds to a halt as the impending death of Mary looms larger and larger. She perceives the approach of death as a positive thing, the ultimate escape from worldly tribulations, and she has dreams about meeting her loved ones again. The novel approaches sentimentality as Mary decides that even in death she can't get home to her beloved Tullamore because her responsibility is to be buried with her husband and daughters at the despised Glasnevin Cemetery. As she trips off across the Elysian fields with her dead daughters and her as yet unborn grandson, it is as though she has been rewarded for her longsuffering, unquestioning acceptance of the social order.

Both Lavin and the critics agree that *The House in Clewe Street* is too long and disjointed, a criticism justified to some extent, at least in the first section, which deals with Gabriel Galloway's origins. However, as David Marshall points out, this is a family tragedy spanning generations, the sort of story that needs room to develop. The novel is in a sense the profile of a town. Like the villages of Lavin's short stories, the town itself may collectively be regarded as a character, so predictable are the strictures and responses of its code. Marshall (in *Commonweal*, July 20, 1945) identifies the village as Trim:

And now Mrs. Lavin has drawn for us a portrait of Trim. She calls it Castlerampart, but it's Trim all right; and it's Trim without false coloring matter. It's Trim under a pale sun when the weather is fine, and under wet, windy skies all the rest of the time. It's Trim seen in a cold light—which is, after all, the authentic light of Ireland.

The book hinges on an understanding both by the readers and characters of the town's code of unspoken social rules or graces. There are three daughters to marry off, and, like Mr. Bennett in *Pride and Prejudice*, Theodore Coniffe must get busy and find someone, preferably for the eldest first. The courtship and marriage in the first section of the novel work in a tight framework of ritual procedure which renders acceptable only marginal deviations from accepted practice, such as Cornelius' falling in love with the youngest daughter instead of the eldest. Everyone knows that a marriage is inevitable. Indeed, to enforce the inevitablility of the event, the first section begins in *medias res* with the father, Theodore, waiting for his daughter and her husband to return from their honeymoon. The question of which daughter got the man is all that remains unanswered.

In the last section of the book, Gabriel will violate the accepted morality of the town and the family by running off with a servant, but impulsiveness will lead to heartaches and the moral code will be redeemed, as Gabriel admits his part in the death of the servant girl, Onny. The novel draws its meaning from this code and the deviations and desperate attempts of Gabriel and Onny to escape from it. Pure submission to the tyranny of the code is exemplified by the second sister, Sara, while the utilitarian use of the code to justify her dictatorial personality is illustrated by the eldest sister, Theresa. Lily, the youngest and the Cinderella figure in the Coniffe family, is given one brief moment of happiness within the social framework of the novel, her marriage to Cornelius and her moment of independence from her eldest sister, before she, like her other sister, Sara, is doomed to a life of servility to the social ethic and Theresa's tyrannical interpretation of it. Of course, all this leads to Gabriel's desperate attempt to escape to the more cosmopolitan world of Dublin.

The sense of rigid social order is augmented by an intense awareness of social class as an irrevocable factor shaping the events of the novel. No one in town except Cornelius is good enough for Theodore Coniffe's daughters. The Coniffe money, earned rather than inherited by Theodore, dictates the family social class— too good to associate with the lower class from which they come, but too self-conscious to do the things which their money will allow them to do. Thus, Cornelius, the new son-in-law who sees the money as a steppingstone to the upper classes, is thrown from his horse and killed trying to emulate those above him.

If the father views upward mobility as the means of triumphing over class structure, then his son exploits his association with the lower class Soraghans, and particularly Onny, to attain freedom from social class conventions. But Gabriel is prevented from attending college, since his aunt feels it is alien to his class; instead he is encouraged to go to bookkeeping school. All of the class mores are heightened by the provincialism of the town and of the sisters themselves, but the conventions are still present—though more subtle—in Dublin. Onny's clothes, her domesticity, her employment and the circumstances of her death are part of a class structure that not even the city can break down. And in the end of the novel Gabriel's decision to tell the entire truth of his relationship to Onny and to face whatever the authorities deem appropriate seems to be a reflection of the morality and class-consciousness of his life on Clewe Street and a triumph of that morality which in turn, for all of its faults, provides Gabriel with an ultimate source of strength and integrity.

Lavin's style, cast in third-person omniscient narration, tends more toward the lyrical in this novel than it usually is in her short stories. The prose of the garden scene, for instance, conveys strong overtones of coming of age in the Garden of Eden.

"Stand up!" said Cornelius, standing up himself, and filled with elation.

Slowly, and as if conscious that in shaking out the folds of the heavily creased tucks in her simple dress she was shaking out the lottery of the years ahead, Lily stood up, and catching the ends of her skirt shook it slowly. The tucks had been for a long time sewn tightly down. Many times they had been pressed closer and tighter by the flatiron; held and thumped and stumped upon the damp ironing board by Mary Ellen's strong hands, so that even now, with the stitches released, they remained for a time in position in spite of the way the girl shook the skirt. Then, as she continued to shake it, the tucks began to give way, heavily and slowly opening, like the tucks in a concertina, and little by little the hemline went lower and lower and lower until at last it reached her ankles and some of the longer, taller grasses reached up as far as it and striped and etched it like a dark embroidery.

The light had vanished from the garden, but stealing away so gradually from them that they had not felt it going, and the white moths and bright-bodied insects that had come out from the bushes dotted the dusk so generously that they did not notice the flowers fading from vision. Having been so near to each other, and so intent upon their task, they seemed still to see each other clearly, but it was probably only the vision of memory; the sight of desire.

"You are no longer a child, Lily," said Cornelius. "You are a woman."

One normally expects the elevation of the dress in such coming-of-age scenes, but Lavin reverses the metaphor by combining it with the image of an unfolding flower. As the dress and the youth who wears it have been held together and restricted by the pressures of convention, in this moment of unveiling, the blossom issues forth. As the flower image fades in the dusk, it is replaced by white moths and bright-bodied insects to complete the moment of escape and the sensuality of the occasion.

Lavin's humor, abundant throughout the novel, also takes a rhetorical turn in her use of a crow simile in the Dickensian caricature of Cornelius:

In fact, in a gathering of normal young people Cornelius looked like a dismal black crow. His long pointed nose resembled a beak, his black hair lay as sleek as feathers. His height caused him to stoop forward and while standing talking he made a habit of gripping a chair back with his long thin fingers. Add to this the fact that, from nervousness, he had developed a habit of looking away from people while addressing them, and therefore, like a bird, he was practically always seen in profile. The final, impossible touch was added to this impression he made of being like a bird when, having an unusually sharp mind, he anticipated what people were about to say, and darting upon their unfinished sentences he picked them up and completed them, giving one the same sensation of nervousness experienced watching a bird in a cage pecking at bird seed, with a sharp bill that may at any moment peck between the bars and stab the unwary fingers without.

There are additional traces of Dickensian humor in the description of the Soraghan household, which remotely echoes Mr. Macawber's, but the principal comic highlight of the book lies in the black humor of the great chariot race of the two rival funeral processions.

We have already discussed Lavin's penchant for black humor, but the comic thrust of the race depends upon the social decorum which pervades the rest of the novel. The local superstition has it that the last to be buried must guard the graves in the cemetery until the arrival of the next corpse. As the funeral procession of Theodore Coniffe approaches the cemetery, a rival procession begins to gallop toward the cemetery from another direction. The race to the gates which ensues is witnessed and cheered on by the spectators, the grave diggers. The fun is greatly enhanced by the unwitting cooperation of the decorum-conscious curate:

But from the furious red of Father Drew's countenance, on which the lather was melting like a snowball on the fire, it was soon clear that it was not from an interest similar to that of Packy Hand's interest in the race that he had leaned out so far and so dangerously. He had, in fact, been leaning out, waving his arms and even frantical-

ly calling out, in a vain effort to stay the unseemly gallop
of the other carriages. But the noise of his voice was not
only drowned by the beating hoofs of the horses and the
rattling rims of the wheels, but worse still his waving arms
were interpreted in several cases to be the fanfaronade
similar to that with which upon other occasions he encouraged the choir to greater vocal velocity. Some timid
souls, who had felt they were actually taking their life
into their hands, urged on their carriages solely because
they believed that in doing so they acted in accord with
the vehement mandate of the clergy. Furthermore, the
horses under the curate's own carriage, hearing all around
them the din of galloping hoofs, and maddened in particular by the sparks that were struck from the steel shoes of
the horses directly in front of them, when they came in
contact with rough stones upon the road, began to increase
their own pace, and hearing the yells of the curate they
remembered their young days and at once entering upon
the competition with the fellow flesh they took a high-
minded aim of being at least in the first six when they
reached the finish, no matter how far away that might be.

The comic incongruity between the indecorousness
of the race and that apotheosis of respectable ritual,
the funeral procession, is another comment upon social
and religious custom. The perversion of the ritual by
local superstition is the perversion of the burial rites
by the local townsfolk, whose ultimate ideas of sanctity
are no more than superstitions. The comic source of
all the ritualistic decorum is, of course, the curate
and the reference to his exhorting the choir to greater
velocity, a metaphor for the fervor with which the
townsfolk are expected to pursue religious devotion
in their everyday lives. But local superstition and custom
pervert his intention and bring about chaos in the

cemetery, just as later in the novel they precipitate Gabriel and Onny's tragedy.

Disruptions in the narrative pattern through editorial intrusion are present in the novel, just as in the early short stories. The reader never completely accustoms himself to it, especially when it takes the form of platitudinous sermonizing, as in the conclusion of the first section:

> Birth and death. In the common pageant of human history, how monotonously these mummers appear.

As the novel progresses, however, such maxims become fewer and less obtrusive.

The House in Clewe Street has three main sections. The first, "Theodore and Cornelius," provides us with the background of the oldest of the three generations of Coniffes, Theodore, and the preliminary exposition of Gabriel's parentage and the background of his environment on Clewe Street.

The middle section is predominantly written from Gabriel's point of view, a David Copperfield sort of *Bildungsroman* about the influences of home and a friend, Sylvester, as well as about Gabriel's developing perceptions of life, especially as they are reflected in the characters of the Soraghan family and the Coniffe sisters.

If part two is predominantly from Gabriel's point of view, and in the main sympathetic to the protagonist, part three corrects any misconceptions we may have had about his moral quality. Gabriel's attitudes and opinions, formed as they were from the prejudices of a provincial town and family and relieved only by his cosmopolitan but slightly Mephistophelian friend, Sylvester, reflect quite accurately the limitations of his perception and his realization of those limitations. As the destiny of the ill-fated lovers is played out, and they discover their chief attraction for each other was the chance for liberation from the dismal life of the town that a love affair offered, Onny flees to other lovers and finally to an abortionist, unable and unwilling to return to the stifling confines of the town or a life circumscribed with a rigid, narrow propriety. Gabriel is not as liberated as Onny, or at least not as willing to go to the same extremes to repudiate his background, and so when he finds out she is pregnant he plans to marry her. When she dies after an abortion he assumes responsibility, although Sylvester has told him that he or another artist might well have been the father. The rightness of Gabriel's action in taking responsibility is tacitly approved by Helen, a figure of moderately acceptable morality (she goes to Mass) who seems to choose socially permissible ways because she sees the rightness in them rather than blindly following some mechanistic social code.

At the center of the novel is the acquisition of self-knowledge by Gabriel. The book concludes with a statement of his realization of his own lack of knowledge, an important final insight for a *Bildungsroman* protagonist:

Dublin lay outstretched below him, its pinnacles gleaming in the morning mists like the pinnacles of a dream. Nothing was seen from this height of the lower reaches of the city—the shops, the tenements, or the busy pavements. They were all huddled together out of sight in the low levels between the tall buildings. But up into the bright air, the steeples, spires, and domes, the lancing pinnacles and towers of church and court and college, rose resplendent, as the city carried aloft her triumphant testimony of man's mighty struggle to cut through ignorance and doubt a path of sane philosophy.

Of this city he knew nothing; he had never seen it, never for one hour been a part of it. He stared down at the fair vista, and at the shining sea beyond it, and for the third time hope rose in his heart, a faint ray perhaps, wan and pale, but as pure and true as the first white javelin of light that pierces the darks of morning.

He held up his head, and strode forward.

In sum, all the religious, social and domestic ties and traps are present in *The House in Clewe Street* as they were in *Mary O'Grady* and so many of Lavin's stories. Perhaps the author herself would not see such entrapment or the social, domestic and religious strictures as particularly horrendous. Rather, in Ireland they are merely the given, those constant elements against which real people and Mary Lavin's characters play out their grim existences.

This study, descriptive rather than evaluative, would never have been undertaken had not Mary Lavin, in my opinion, deserved the accolades and awards that have been bestowed upon her work. There are few living writers in Ireland, and none among the short-story writers, who measure up to her standard. That her work has not received the critical attention it deserves is due in some measure to the precision and clarity of her style and vision, which embarrass criticism and offer little to occupy the attention of contemporary textual explicators. The verisimilitude of her stories and characters renders her work clear and at the same time significant to the reader. But such clarity and craftsmanship in style and structure are the products of a writer of the first rank, a position which Mary Lavin had achieved in Ireland thirty years ago and has held ever since.

Bibliography

1. BOOKS

At Sallygap and Other Stories. Boston: Little, Brown & Co., 1947.

The Becker Wives and Other Stories. London: Michael Joseph, Ltd., 1946.

The Becker Wives. New York: New American Library, 1971.

Collected Stories. Boston: Houghton Mifflin Co., 1971.

The Great Wave and Other Stories. London and New York: Macmillan, 1961.

Happiness and Other Stories. London: Constable, 1969.

The House in Clewe Street. Boston: Little, Brown & Co., 1945; London: Michael Joseph, Ltd., 1945.

In the Middle of the Fields. London: Constable, 1967; New York: Macmillan, 1969.

A Likely Story. New York: Macmillan, 1957; Dublin: Dolmen Press, 1967.

The Long Ago and Other Stories. London: Michael Joseph, Ltd., 1944.

Mary O'Grady. Boston: Little, Brown & Co., 1950; London: Michael Joseph, Ltd., 1950.

A Memory and Other Stories. Boston: Houghton Mifflin Co., 1973.

The Patriot Son and Other Stories. London: Michael Joseph, Ltd., 1956.

The Second Best Children in the World. Boston: Houghton Mifflin Co., 1972.

Selected Stories. Preface: Mary Lavin. New York: Macmillan, 1959.

A Single Lady and Other Stories. London: Michael Joseph, Ltd., 1951.

Stories of Mary Lavin. London: Constable, 1964.

Tales from Bective Bridge. Boston: Little, Brown & Co., 1942; London: Michael Joseph, Ltd., 1943.

2. SHORT STORIES PUBLISHED SEPARATELY ONLY

"Daggle-Tail." *Pick of the Litter: Betty Cavanna's Favorite Dog Stories*. London: Westminster Press, 1952.

"The Girders." *The Strand Magazine* 107 (May 1944): 62–67.

"The Rabbit." *American Mercury* 57 (November 1943): 564–71.

"Story of the Widow's Son." *Forty-four Irish Short Stories: An Anthology of Irish Short Fiction from Yeats to Frank O'Connor*. Edited by Devin Adair Garrity. Dublin: Devin-Adair, 1955.

"Tom." *The New Yorker* 48 (January 20, 1973): 34–42.

"Trastevere." *The New Yorker* 47 (December 11, 1971): 43–51.

3. NOVEL SERIALIZED

Gabriel Galloway (later published under title of *The House in Clewe Street*). *Atlantic Monthly* 174 (November 1944): 155–64; (December 1944): 159–68; 175 (January 1945): 125–40; (February 1945): 139–48; (March 1945): 139–48; (April 1945): 143–52; (May 1945): 139–48.

4. POEMS

"Let Me Come Inland Always." *Dublin Magazine* 15 (January–March 1940): 1–2.

"Poem." *Dublin Magazine* 15 (January–March 1940): 2.

5. ESSAY

"Preface," *Selected Stories*. New York: Macmillan, 1959, pp. v–viii.

6. BOOK REVIEW

Review of *Some Curious People* by Brinsley MacNamara. *The Bell* 10 (September 1945): 547–49.

7. MAJOR CRITICAL AND OTHER MATERIAL ON MARY LAVIN

Bryant, Byron R. "The Great Wave and Other Stories." *Ramparts* 1 (September 1962): 94–95.

Caswell, Robert W. "The Human Heart's Vagaries." *Kilkenny Review* 12–13 (Spring 1965): 69–89.

———. "Irish Political Reality and Mary Lavin's *Tales from Bective Bridge.*" *Éire-Ireland* 3, no. 1 (Spring 1968): 48–60.

———. "Mary Lavin: Breaking a Pathway." *Dublin Magazine* 6 (1967): 32–44.

Driscoll, Joanne. "Mary Lavin and the Irish Split-Personality." *The Critic* 22 (December 1963-January 1964): 20–23.

Dunsany, Lord. "A Preface," *Tales from Bective Bridge*. London: Michael Joseph, Ltd., 1943. pp. 5–8.

Fremantle, Anne. "A Certain Craft." (Review of *Selected Stories*.) *Commonweal* 70 (September 18, 1959): 523–24.

Hackett, Francis. "First Novel." (Commentary on *The House in Clewe Street*.) *On Judging Books*. New York: John Day Co., 1947. pp. 271–74.

Hughes, Riley. "And, for some light . . . " (Includes review of *At Sallygap and Other Stories*.) *America* 76 (March 29, 1947): 720–21.

Kiely, Benedict. *Modern Irish Fiction: A Critique*. Dublin: Golden Eagle Books, Ltd., 1950. pp. 57–58, 92–93.

Macken, Mary M. "Fiction." (Review of *The Long Ago and Other Stories*.) *Studies* 33 (September 1944): 428.

Marshall, David. *"The House in Clewe Street." Commonweal* 42 (July 20, 1945): 340–41.

Martin, Augustine. "A Skeleton Key to the Stories of Mary Lavin." *Studies* 52 (Winter 1963): 393–406.

"Mary Lavin." *Wilson Library Bulletin* 20 (November 1945): 188.

Murphy, C. A. *Imaginative Vision and Story Art in Three Irish Writers, Sean O'Faolain, Mary Lavin, and Frank O'Connor.* Dissertation, Trinity College, Dublin, 1968.

Murray, Thomas J. "Mary Lavin's World: Lovers and Strangers." *Éire-Ireland* 7 (1972): 122–31.

O'Connor, Frank. *The Lonely Voice: A Study of the Short Story.* Cleveland and New York: World, 1963. pp. 202–13.

———. "The Girl at the Gaol Gate." *A Review of English Literature* 1 (April 1960): 25–33.

O'Faolain, Sean. *"The House in Clewe Street." The Bell* 12 (April 1946): 81–82.

Peden, William. "Stories of the Quarter." (Includes review of *Selected Stories.*) *Story* NS 33 (1960): 214–15.

Plant, Richard R. "Lavin . . . " (Review of *Tales from Bective Bridge.*) *Saturday Review of Literature* 25 (June 6, 1942): 9–10.

Prescott, Orville. "Books of *The Times.*" (Review of *The Great Wave and Other Stories.*) *New York Times,* August 2, 1961, p. 27.

———. "Books of *The Times.*" (Review of *Selected Stories.*) *New York Times,* June 15, 1959, p. 25.

Pritchett, V. S. "Introduction." *Collected Stories.* Boston: Houghton Mifflin Co., 1971. Pp. ix–xiii.

"The Quiet Authoress." *Irish Sunday Press* (Dublin), April 21, 1968, p. 20.

Roark, B. J. *Mary Lavin: The Local and the Universal.* Dissertation, University of Colorado, 1968.

Rooney, Philip. *"The Becker Wives and Other Stories." The Irish Monthly* 75 (January 1947): 44–45.

Ryan, Stephen. "*Selected Stories.*" *The Critic* 18 (August-September 1959): 38.

Weeks, Edward. "The Peripatetic Reviewer." (Includes review of *Selected Stories.*) *Atlantic Monthly* 204 (August 1959): 78–79.

Whitaker, Thomas. "Vision and Voice in Some Recent Fiction." (Includes review of *The Great Wave and Other Stories.*) *Minnesota Review* 2 (Winter 1962): 247–48.

8. BIBLIOGRAPHY

Doyle, Paul A. "Mary Lavin: A Checklist." *The Papers of the Bibliographical Society of America* 63 (1969): 317–21.